Making Connections

Reading Comprehension Skills and Strategies

Book 3

EDUCATORS PUBLISHING SERVICE
Cambridge and Toronto

Contents

Unit 1: Sequencing

Theme: **San Francisco**

Text 1:	Changing San Francisco	4–5
	Changing San Francisco Activities	6–7
Text 2:	Golden Gate Bridge	8–9
	Golden Gate Bridge Activities	10–11
Text 3:	San Francisco Earthquake	12–14
	San Francisco Earthquake Activities	15
Text 4:	Transportation in San Francisco	16
	Transportation in San Francisco Activities	17

Unit 2: Main Idea

Theme: **Heroes**

Text 1:	Jack's Report	18–19
	Jack's Report Activities	20–21
Text 2:	Jesse Owens	22–23
	Jesse Owens Activities	24–25
Text 3:	Florence Nightingale	26–28
	Florence Nightingale Activities	29
Text 4:	Sally Ride: American Hero	30
	Sally Ride: American Hero Activities	31

Unit 3: Compare and Contrast

Theme: **United States and Australia**

Text 1:	Pen Pals	32–33
	Pen Pals Activities	34–35
Text 2:	Holiday or Vacation?	36–37
	Holiday or Vacation? Activities	38–39
Text 3:	Above and Below	40–42
	Above and Below Activities	43
Text 4:	Sports Talk	44
	Sports Talk Activities	45

Unit 4: Drawing Conclusions/Predicting Outcomes

Theme: **Fables**

Text 1:	Who Was Aesop?	46–47
	Who Was Aesop? Activities	48–49
Text 2:	The Lion and the Mouse	50–51
	The Lion and the Mouse Activities	52–53
Text 3:	The Tortoise and the Hare	54–56
	The Tortoise and the Hare Activities	57
Text 4:	The Ant and the Grasshopper	58
	The Ant and the Grasshopper Activities	59

Unit 5: Fact and Opinion

Theme: **Environmental Issues**

Text 1:	Sunny Waters	60–61
	Sunny Waters Activities	62–63
Text 2:	Glass: Let's Save It!	64–65
	Glass: Let's Save It! Activities	66–67
Text 3:	The Daily Spin	68–70
	The Daily Spin Activities	71
Text 4:	That's Rubbish!	72
	That's Rubbish! Activities	73

Unit 6: Cause and Effect

Theme: **Citizenship**

Text 1:	How to Celebrate the Fourth of July	74–75
	How to Celebrate the Fourth of July Activities	76–77
Text 2:	A Terrible Mess	78–79
	A Terrible Mess Activities	80–81
Text 3:	Forgetful Sam	82–84
	Forgetful Sam Activities	85
Text 4:	Splat!	86
	Splat! Activities	87

Unit 1

Sequencing Sequencing is putting things in the order in which they happened.

Changing San Francisco

In 1848, a man named James Marshall discovered a few tiny gold nuggets in a river in California. The California Gold Rush began! At this time, San Francisco was a small town on a large bay. Steamships and trading ships crossed the bay. In town, the buildings were small and made of wood.

> What sequence of events made San Francisco a wealthy city?

In just two years, over 90,000 people from all over the world came to California to search for gold. The small town had become a busy city. San Francisco grew so fast that some people had to live in canvas tents. Many stores were set up in tents as well.

The gold rush ended in 1854. By 1856, San Francisco had become a bustling city, with a population of 30,000. Many people who made a fortune from gold built large stone and brick houses. Multistory buildings sprang up.

By the early 1900s, San Francisco's population was almost 400,000. As San Francisco grew, so did the need for new forms of transportation. In 1937, the Golden Gate Bridge opened. People were able to drive cars across the bay instead of taking ferries.

Today, skyscrapers create an impressive skyline, and the city covers forty-nine square miles. Huge container ships load and unload their cargo onto docks in the bay. San Francisco is a beautiful, modern city, with a population of more than 790,000.

Practice the Skill

Sequence with a Timeline

Fill in the missing dates.

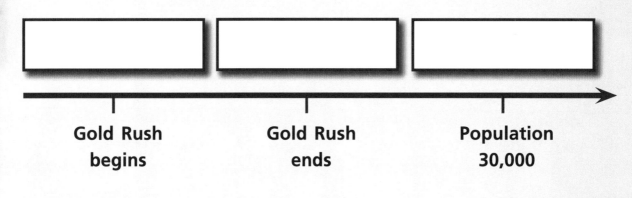

| Gold Rush begins | Gold Rush ends | Population 30,000 |

Before or After 1900?

Put the following details into the correct column to show when they happened.

- steamships
- container ships
- cars over bridge
- wooden buildings

- skyscrapers
- fortunes from gold
- brick houses

Before 1900	After 1900

Identify Details

Write two or three details in each box.

<table>
<tr>
<td>

1848 San Francisco

_____

_____

_____

</td>
<td>

1800s ships

_____

_____

_____

</td>
</tr>
</table>

San Francisco

<table>
<tr>
<td>

1900s San Francisco

_____

_____

_____

</td>
<td>

San Francisco today

_____

_____

_____

</td>
</tr>
</table>

Golden Gate Bridge

What sequence of events delayed the building of the Golden Gate Bridge?

San Francisco's Golden Gate Bridge is one of the most famous bridges in the world. It spans the Golden Gate Strait, a narrow strip of water between San Francisco Bay and the Pacific Ocean. Before the bridge was built, the only way to cross the strait was by boat.

Talks about building a bridge began in 1872. However, it took almost fifty years for someone to work out how it could be done. In 1921, Joseph Strauss drew up his first plans for the Golden Gate Bridge. However, not everyone liked Strauss's plans, so they were changed.

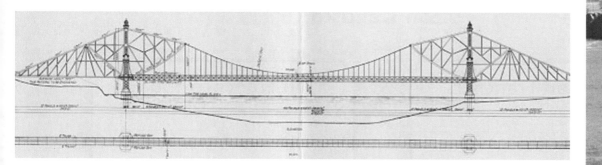

Joseph Strauss's plan for the Golden Gate Bridge

Plans for the bridge were finished in 1930. Because of the size of the project, it took two and a half years to start construction. The construction team had to organize money to pay for the bridge. They also had to find the best builders for the bridge. Finally, construction began in January, 1933.

First, the workers built huge concrete blocks. On top of the blocks, they built high steel towers. After that, the workers stretched thick steel ropes called main cables between the towers. Then they connected smaller cables to the main cables. These cables all worked to hold the bridge up. Finally, they built the road.

It took almost four and a half years to build the Golden Gate Bridge. On May 28, 1937, the first cars crossed it. Now about 115,000 vehicles cross the bridge every day!

Practice the Skill

Golden Gate Bridge Timeline

Fill in the date to match each event on the flow chart.

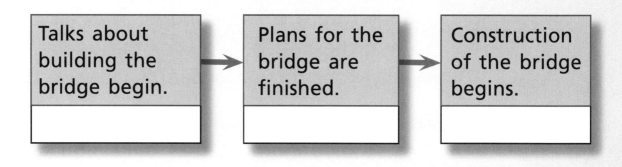

Talks about building the bridge begin.	Plans for the bridge are finished.	Construction of the bridge begins.

Sequence of Events

Number these events in order.

- ☐ Steel towers were built.
- ☐ The road was built.
- ☐ Smaller cables were connected to the main cables.
- ☐ Huge concrete blocks were built.
- ☐ Main cables were stretched between the towers.

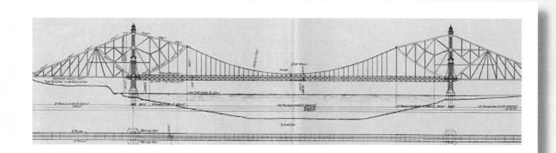

Facts and Details

Find the information in the text to complete the following sentences.

There was no bridge across the strait until 1937,

so

```
                        .
```

People didn't like Strauss's first plans,

so

```
                        .
```

It took two and a half years to start building the bridge

because

```
                        .
```

Writing

Why do you think that building the bridge was so important?

San Francisco Earthquake

On what day do you think the scariest sequence of events occurred?

April 18, 1906

When I woke up, my bed was moving! Books were falling off the shelves. I pulled the covers over my head. Then I heard Mom and Dad calling me.

I jumped up, and we raced downstairs. Some of the furniture had fallen over. Mom's favorite plates were all smashed on the floor.

I could hear dogs howling outside, so I ran over to the window. The sun was just coming up. I could see big cracks and holes in the pavement. Some houses had fallen down! Dad went outside. People in their nightclothes were out in the street.

Everyone was yelling and crying. When Dad came back, he told us there was an earthquake, maybe the biggest earthquake ever!

April 19, 1906

Everyone is shaken up. This earthquake was really, really bad. We still feel little tremors every now and again. Huge fires are burning everywhere. Houses on our street have burned down. There's no electricity or gas. I heard Dad talking to the mayor. He told Dad that there's more damage from the fires than from the earthquake itself.

I miss my friends, and I'm worried about them. There's no school so I don't know how everyone is doing. Most of the stores aren't open. Mom has to wait in line to get food. Then she has to cook on a little fire out in the street. It's hard living like this.

San Francisco Chronicle.

SAN FRANCISCO CHRONICLE, SUNDAY, APRIL 22, 1906.

VOL. LXXXVIII.

FORCE OF THE FIRE IS AT LAST SPEN
BANKS ABLE TO MEET THE EMERGEN

PLENTY OF MONEY IN THE VAULTS

Financiers Want Thirty Days in Which to Put Affairs in Shape for Business

THIRTY DAYS OF HOLIDAY.

Governor Pardee yesterday, after a confer-
financiers, agreed to declare a legal
day as long as the emer-
Governor will confer

Long Hard Battle on Near Water From Are Sav

The fire is out. Only smoking, smoldering embers remain. The finish was at the grain warehouse and United States bonded warehouse in the block bounded by Sansome and Battery streets. Telegraph Hill and the bay. There the fire that swept to the

April 20, 1906

There's still no electricity so there are no lights. The mayor said everyone should stay indoors at night. The fires look spooky in the dark. Soldiers and police are helping to fight the fires. Lots of people are hurt, and the hospitals are full.

April 22, 1906

Lots of people don't have homes or belongings anymore. They are living in tents. Soldiers are giving them food and blankets.

Thousands of volunteers are helping to get things back to normal. We are starting to rebuild our city. However, it will take a lot of time.

Practice the Skill

Earthquake Timeline

Put the following events in the correct order on the timeline.
- earthquake starts
- soldiers and police fight fires
- huge fires burn
- homeless live in tents

April 18

April 19

April 20

April 22

Events Inside and Outside

List in order two events that happened inside the house. Then list two events that happened outside.

Inside

1. _____

2. _____

Outside

1. _____

2. _____

Transportation in San Francisco

In what sequence did transportation improve in San Francisco?

As the city of San Francisco grew, people needed more efficient ways to travel. In the 1840s, people rode in horse-drawn vehicles, such as buggies and wagons. The roads were made of dirt, and riding around was very bumpy and uncomfortable. By 1850, people used boats and ferries to get to different places around the bay.

Transportation improved by the early 1900s. People traveled by bicycle, motorcar, and trolley. In 1937, the Golden Gate Bridge was built, so people could drive across the bay. By this time, roads were made of tar, which made riding smooth and comfortable.

By 1946, many people had cars. The bridges around the bay became clogged with traffic. A plan was made to build a public transportation system. The subway system, known as BART, carried its first passengers in 1972.

Practice the Skill

Transportation Sequence

What new form of transportation was used in these years?

1840s ———

1850s ———

early 1900s ———

1972 ———

Road Changes

Write two details about roads for these dates.

1840s _____

_____

1937 _____

_____

The Subway

The subway system was built because _____

_____

_____

_____ .

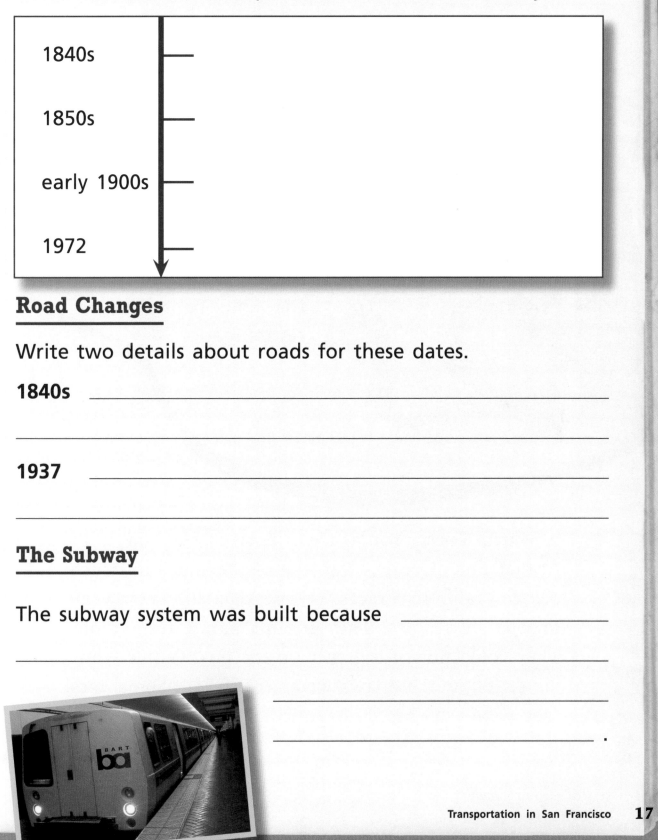

Unit 2

Main Idea   The main ideas are the most important ideas or information in a text.

Jack's Report

What did Martin Luther King Jr. care about most?

Jack was nervous. He had to give a report to his class. His report was about Martin Luther King Jr., the American civil rights leader.

Martin Luther King Jr. was born in Georgia in 1929. At that time, Georgia was one of the states in which people of different races were segregated. They went to separate schools. They ate in separate restaurants. They could not sit together on the bus. People who didn't follow these laws were sent to jail. Sometimes, they were even beaten or killed.

Martin Luther King Jr. knew that treating people differently because of their race was not right. He wanted all Americans to be free to live, work, and go to school together.

Martin Luther King Jr. asked people to help him in a peaceful way. He had a dream that one day children of any race would be able to walk together as friends.

People worked for many years to change the laws. In 1954, the law was changed. Black children and white children were finally able to go to the same schools.

Today, Martin Luther King Jr. is remembered as a great leader. People are still working to make his dream come true.

Jack finished his talk and smiled. He asked if his classmates had any questions. Many hands shot up.

Practice the Skill

Main Ideas in Sequence

Number these main ideas in the order
they appear in Jack's report.

☐ Children of both races were finally able
to go to the same schools.

☐ Martin Luther King Jr. wanted to change the laws in
a peaceful way.

☐ People of different races were kept apart.

☐ Martin Luther King Jr. wanted all Americans to be free.

What King Wanted

Read the main ideas above. Choose two of them to
tell what Martin Luther King Jr. wanted.

1. _____

_____

_____.

2. _____

_____

_____.

Identify Details

Find three details in the text that support the following main idea.

People of different races were separated.

1. _____
   _____

2. _____
   _____

3. _____
   _____

Vocabulary

Find words in the text that mean

- "with one another" _____
- "ended" _____
- "places to eat" _____
- "set apart; separated" _____

Jesse Owens

Why was Jesse Owens so famous?

James Cleveland Owens was born in Alabama in 1913. He was the grandson of a slave. When he was eight, his family moved to Cleveland, Ohio. They were very poor and wanted a better life.

At his new school, a teacher misheard his name (J. C.) and began calling him Jesse. The new name stuck. Jesse took on small jobs to help his family. He was so busy with work and school that he often ran from place to place to get things done. Jesse enjoyed running and was good at it, too!

Jesse became a track star in high school and college. At a track meet in 1935, he set three world records in running and long jump, and tied for another. No one in the world had won so many medals at a meet before! Even though Jesse was a star, many people treated him with prejudice because he was African American.

Jesse entered the 1936 Olympic Games in Germany. He won gold medals in the 100-meter race, the 200-meter race, and the long jump. His 400-meter relay team also won gold. Jesse showed the world that people of all races should have a chance to compete.

After the Olympics, Jesse continued to race. He would give other runners a ten-yard start, and still beat them! As his fame grew, Jesse became a public speaker. He retired from racing in 1971.

Although Jesse was famous, he always tried to help young athletes. In 1976, he received the Medal of Freedom from the President of the United States. Jesse Owens overcame many challenges to become one of the most famous athletes in history.

Practice the Skill

Write Main Ideas

Find the main idea for paragraphs one to five. The third one has been done for you.

1

_____

_____

2

_____

_____

3

___Jesse Owens became a famous track star.___

_____

4

_____

_____

5

_____

_____

Sequence with a Timeline

Fill in the timeline.

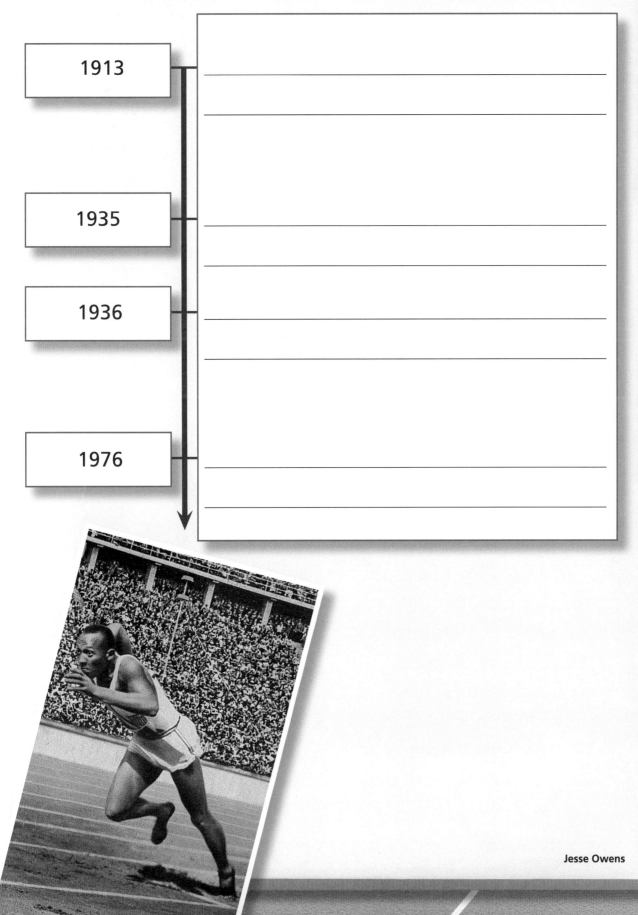

1913

1935

1936

1976

Florence Nightingale

Do you ever think about what you want to be when you grow up? Florence Nightingale did. She always wanted to be a nurse.

How did Florence Nightingale achieve her goal?

Florence was born in Italy in 1820 and grew up in England. Most girls did not study math or science at that time, but Florence loved these subjects. Her father decided to teach them to her. She was a very good student.

As a young woman, Florence visited sick people in local villages. She also went to hospitals to watch nurses work. She was interested in how hospitals were run. In 1851, Florence went to Germany to train as a nurse. She returned home to work in a hospital in London. Florence continued to learn about nursing.

In 1854, England went to war with Russia. Many soldiers were wounded and needed help. Florence Nightingale took nurses to the army hospital in the Crimea to look after the soldiers.

When Florence returned to England, she was a hero. She had changed the way the army hospital was run. She wanted to change other hospitals, too. In 1860, Florence Nightingale started a school for nurses.

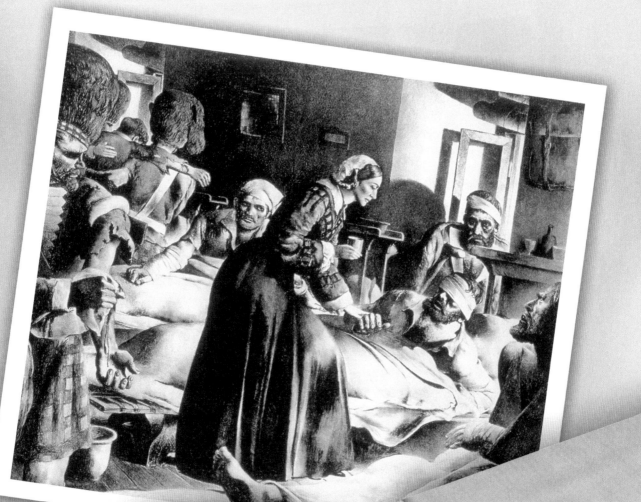

Florence knew that sick people often got worse in hospitals. Germs were spread from one person to another. In that time, doctors and nurses didn't wash their hands or their equipment very well. Florence worked with them to make sure all the instruments and the hospital rooms were clean. This helped stop germs from spreading.

Florence Nightingale lived to be ninety years old. She spent her life helping others. Florence's work changed the way hospitals were run in countries around the world.

Practice the Skill

Main Ideas

Write the main idea for paragraphs one to six.

1 _____

_____

2 _____

_____

3 _____

_____

4 _____

_____

5 _____

_____

6 _____

_____

Check Comprehension

What did Florence Nightingale start in 1860?

_____

_____

Writing

What do you think was the most important thing Florence Nightingale did?

Sally Ride:
American Hero

Why is Sally Ride famous?

Sally Ride was born on May 26, 1951, in California. When she was young, Sally liked school and sports. She played baseball, football, and tennis. When she was ten years old, Sally won a place on the U.S. Junior Tennis Circuit.

After high school, Sally studied at Stanford University. She earned four degrees, including a master's in physics. Sally was a very clever student.

In 1978, Sally Ride applied for a position with NASA. More than 8,000 people applied. Sally was one of the thirty-five chosen. Only six were women.

After years of training, in 1983, Sally orbited the earth on the space shuttle *Challenger*. She was the first American woman in space!

Sally Ride flew on one more mission in 1984. She now teaches at the University of California. Sally also hosts festivals and workshops for middle-school girls. She knows it is important for girls to enjoy math, science, and technology.

Practice the Skill

Main Ideas

Write the main idea for each paragraph.

1 _____

_____

2 _____

_____

3 _____

_____

4 _____

_____

5 _____

_____

Summarize

Use the main ideas above to help you summarize the
newspaper report.

_____

_____

_____

_____

Unit 3

Compare and Contrast To figure out how things are alike and how they are different.

Pen Pals

> What do you think is the biggest difference between Cheyenne and Sydney?

INBOX

To	talisha@austmail.com.au
From	brad@usmail.com
Sent	January 15, 2006
Subject	Hello!

Hi Talisha,

In class today, I picked your name as an e-mail pen pal. I'm so excited to be writing to someone in Australia!

It's winter here in Cheyenne, Wyoming. We have sunny days, but it's really cold. My family likes to go to the mountains where there is almost always snow.

Last weekend, my grandpa took my mom and me out snowmobiling. We had a really fun time. Mom bought me a new winter hat and mittens to wear. I don't really like winter hats, but at least it keeps my head warm. I wore sunscreen on my nose so I wouldn't get sunburned. Did you know that you have to watch out for sunburn in the snow?!

When we came home, we had dinner, then Mom started a fire in the fireplace. For dessert we made s'mores by toasting marshmallows in the fire, then making a sandwich with two graham crackers and a piece of chocolate. The warm marshmallow melts the chocolate. Yum! Winter is the best :)

Your friend,
Brad

To	brad@usmail.com
From	talisha@austmail.com.au
Sent	January 17, 2006
Subject	Re: Hello!

Hi Brad,

It was great to get your message! It will be fun to have an e-mail pen friend from the United States.

It's summer in Sydney, so the weather is hot and sunny. Yesterday, my dad took me to the beach. We had a great time in the ocean. We went for a ride on a motorboat that raced across the waves. It was lots of fun!

I have a new sun hat. I love it. It helps keep the sun off my head and neck. I'm amazed that you were wearing sunscreen in winter! I wore sunscreen on my nose, too! It's easy to get sunburned on the water.

After our ride, we cooked sausages on the barbecue, and then went out for ice cream. It was great. I just love summer.

Write back soon.

Your friend,
Talisha

P.S. I've never heard of s'mores before.

Practice the Skill

What Looks the Same? What Looks Different?

Look at these drawings of Brad and Talisha. Write two things that are the same, and three that are different.

Same

_____

_____

Different

_____

_____

_____

Compare and Contrast

Fill in this Venn diagram about what Brad and Talisha write in their e-mails.

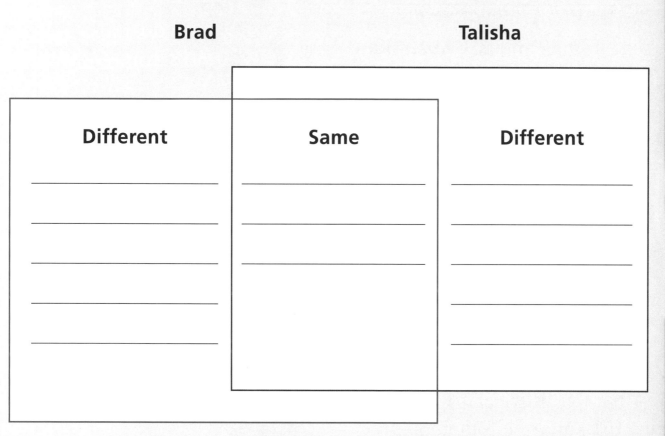

Brad   **Talisha**

Different   **Same**   **Different**

Vocabulary

Find three words or phrases that have the word "sun" in them.

_____

_____

_____

Holiday or Vacation?

How do these two parks compare?

Tomás and his Australian cousin, Sarah, were driving through Yellowstone National Park. "Guess what?" Tomás boasted. "Yellowstone is the oldest national park in the United States and the world. It was founded in 1872."

"Well, Royal Park, near Sydney, is the second oldest," Sarah responded. "It was founded in 1879, so Yellowstone is only a few years older!"

"I bet Yellowstone is bigger than your park, too," said Tomás. "It covers 3,468 square miles!"

"You win again!" laughed Sarah. "Royal Park covers 151 square kilometers, and kilometers are shorter than miles."

Tomás and Sarah stopped at the entrance to a hiking trail, where they saw a park ranger. "Is this a good trail for spotting wildlife?" Tomás asked.

"Sure," the ranger replied. "Plenty of elk, bison, moose, beavers, wolves, and bears live in Yellowstone," he said. "Remember, they may look cute, but some of them can be very dangerous. Always keep your distance, and don't try to feed them! It is also very important that you don't pick any flowers in this park."

The two cousins started off on the trail. "You can't pick flowers at Royal Park either. And you can't feed the animals, but not because they're dangerous," Sarah said. "Human food can make the wallabies, platypuses, koalas, and wombats really sick."

"You won't find those animals at Yellowstone! I've never seen a live wallaby," said Tomás. "And I've never even heard of a wombat! What is that?"

"You'll have to find out when we go to Royal Park in Australia next holidays," Sarah replied.

"You mean next vacation," said Tomás. "I can't wait!"

Practice the Skill

Park Animals

List four different animals found in each park.

Royal Park

_____

_____

_____

_____

Yellowstone

_____

_____

_____

_____

National Park Rules

List two rules that are the same in both parks.

National Park Rules

_____

_____

_____

_____

Identify Details

Complete the table.

	Yellowstone Park	Royal Park
Size:		
Year founded:		
Country:		

Check Comprehension

Write T (true) or F (false) in the boxes.

Kilometers are longer than miles. ☐

Yellowstone is older than Royal Park. ☐

Human food is good for animals. ☐

Vocabulary

What does "keep your distance" mean?

_____

_____

_____

Above and Below

Some people live in apartments high above the ground. You may live in a tall apartment building yourself. But do you know anyone who lives underground? In Coober Pedy, a town in the very hot Australian desert, people do.

What do you think is so different about living underground?

Why would anyone live underground? In Coober Pedy, it's because living above ground is very hot. In the summer, the temperature reaches 120 degrees Fahrenheit! Above-ground homes in Coober Pedy need air conditioning all year round. But under the ground, the temperature is never more than 79 degrees Fahrenheit. The air is cooler because the heat of the sun cannot get through the rocks.

In Coober Pedy, people found out that it was cool underground when they were looking for precious stones called opals. People began digging for opals in Coober Pedy in the early 1900s. They dug tunnels and caves and noticed that the caves were cooler than their homes. Many people moved out of their hot houses and into empty caves.

Coober Pedy

Today, underground homes in Coober Pedy have kitchens, bathrooms, and bedrooms, just like apartments above the ground. People can cook, clean, eat, and sleep in both types of homes. Just as houses and apartments come in different sizes, underground homes can be large or small.

Although some underground homes have skylights, they don't have windows. People need to turn on more lights in the daytime in a Coober Pedy underground home than in an above-ground apartment.

An underground living room

You can't grow a garden underground because plants need sunlight. You can't grow a garden in an apartment because apartments have too little outdoor space.

If an apartment is not big enough, the people living there have to move. But if an underground home isn't big enough, the people who live there can just dig another room!

Practice the Skill

Same and Different

What is the same and what is different about living in an above-ground apartment and living underground?

Different	Same	Different
Above		**Below**

Details about Coober Pedy

Fill in the diagram.

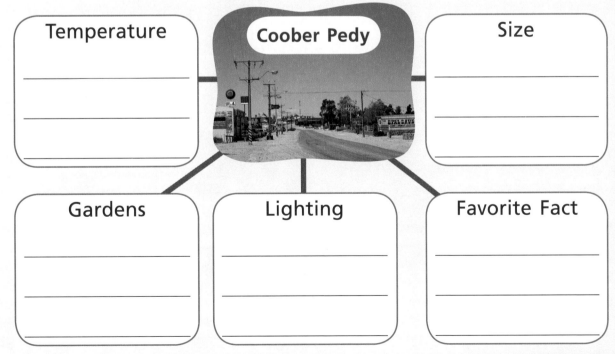

Temperature

Coober Pedy

Size

Gardens

Lighting

Favorite Fact

Sports Talk

Did you know the most popular sport in the United States is baseball? Baseball is played outdoors on a grassy field that has four bases in a diamond shape. Games are played by two teams of nine players each. Players score runs by hitting a ball with a rounded bat, then running around three bases to the fourth base, which is called home plate. Players wear uniforms if they play for a school or Little League team.

What are the differences between baseball and cricket?

Cricket is popular in Australia. Like baseball, it is played with two teams. However, each team has eleven players. Cricket is played on a grassy field. Players hit a ball with a flat bat. Instead of running around bases, players score runs by running between two wickets. Players wear uniforms if they play for a school or club.

Practice the Skill

What's the Same?

List what is the same about baseball and cricket.

_____

_____

_____

_____

Something Different

In baseball, players run around _____,

but in cricket, players run between _____ .

Scoreboard

Fill in the details about each game.

Where

Cricket: _____

Baseball: _____

Bat

Cricket: _____

Baseball: _____

Number of teams

Cricket: _____

Baseball: _____

Number of players

Cricket: _____

Baseball: _____

Number of wickets

Cricket: _____

Number of bases

Baseball: _____

Unit 4

Drawing Conclusions/Predicting Outcomes Combine information from a text with what is already known to build additional meaning.

Who Was Aesop?

Aesop's fables are known and loved around the world. Yet very little is known about the man who told these stories. Aesop is thought to have been a slave in ancient Greece. He was born more than 2,500 years ago, in about 620 BCE. Aesop was a wise man. His master admired him for his wisdom. At that time, a master could free a slave whom he admired.

Aesop told stories because, in those days, very few people could read or write. When stories were good and well told, people would remember them and retell them. This is how they were passed along.

> How do you know Aesop was freed?

Aesop's stories were simple, but they were good and well told. They were about animals that could talk. The animals made mistakes. A king asked Aesop to tell his stories to some important people. The stories had advice that the king wanted the people to follow.

Aesop may not have made up all the fables himself. Some may have been older stories that he retold. But even if he did not make them up, Aesop made them famous by telling them so well. The first time Aesop's stories were written down was almost 300 years after his death. We still read and enjoy Aesop's fables after more than 2,500 years.

Why are Aesop's stories still popular today?

Practice the Skill

Conclusions about Aesop

Read the following details about Aesop. Then answer the questions to draw conclusions.

Aesop was a wise slave.	His master admired his wisdom.	Masters could free slaves they admired.

What do you think happened to Aesop?

_____

_____

Stories were told rather than written down because people couldn't read.	Stories were retold if they were good.

What do you think happened to Aesop's stories?

_____

_____

The king wanted to give people advice.	The king wanted Aesop to help him.

What do you think Aesop did?

_____

_____

Stories that Last

1. Do you think children in the future will still read Aesop's fables? Why?

_____

_____

_____

_____

_____

2. Name a story and tell why you think it will be read in the future.

_____

_____

_____

_____

_____

Listen or Read?

Would you rather listen to stories or read them yourself? Why?

_____

_____

_____

The Lion and the Mouse

One day, a little mouse was hurrying through the forest. In her rush, she ran straight across a lion's nose, waking the lion from his nap.

How do you know the lion and the mouse got along?

The startled lion swiftly placed his huge paw across the mouse's tail. He roared with fury, opening his mouth wide.

"Oh, noble king of the forest," squeaked the trembling mouse. "Please forgive me for waking you! If you will spare me, I shall never forget it. One day, I might be able to help you."

The lion was very amused by what the little mouse had said. "Oh, you are very brave to plead with the king of the forest," the lion said, laughing.

Shall I free her or not? he thought. The lion lifted his paw from the mouse's tail.

A few days later, the mouse heard a terrible roar that echoed throughout the forest. The roar sounded very familiar.

The mouse ran through the forest toward the sound. The lion was caught in a hunter's net! Using her sharp teeth, the mouse began gnawing through the ropes of the net.

Before long, the mouse chewed a hole large enough to free the mighty lion. "Thank you, thank you," said the lion. "You have saved my life."

"Sometimes, even a tiny mouse can save a mighty lion," said the mouse, smiling.

Practice the Skill

Draw Conclusions

Finish the following sentences.

The mouse ran across the lion's nose because _____

_____ .

When the lion had his paw on the mouse's tail, the mouse was feeling _____

_____

_____ .

Predict Outcomes

1. If the mouse had called the lion a cruel monster, what do you think the lion would have done?

_____

_____

2. What do you think a real lion would have done?

_____

_____

Sequence the Events

Number these story events in order.

- ☐ The lion is free.
- ☐ The mouse saw the lion in the net.
- ☐ The mouse heard a roar.
- ☐ The mouse gnawed the ropes.

Lesson of the Story

If the lion said, "I've learned an important lesson today," what would that lesson be?

_____

_____

_____

Vocabulary

Draw pictures to show what these phrases mean.

roaring with fury

trembling with fear

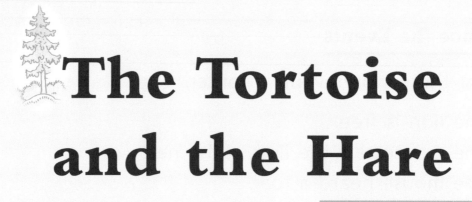

The Tortoise and the Hare

Tortoise and Hare were friends who lived near a very big hill. Hare, with his long, strong legs, could run up the hill and then down again in sixty seconds. Tortoise, with his short, stubby legs, could not move very fast. It took him a very long time to get anywhere.

> **Which animal should win the race?**

Hare always teased Tortoise about how slowly he walked. Tortoise was sick and tired of Hare's teasing, so one day he challenged Hare to a race.

"This is a joke! You've got to be kidding," Hare said with a laugh. "I can run circles around you. You'll never beat me!"

"We'll see," said Tortoise.

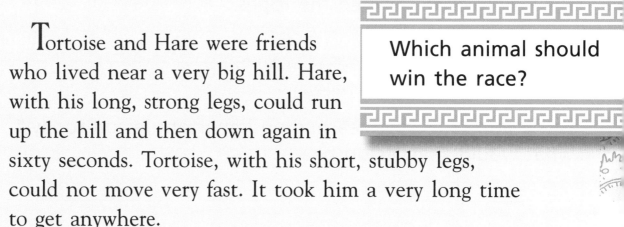

Hare and Tortoise lined up and the race began! Hare ran like the wind and was soon out of sight. Tortoise plodded along slowly and steadily. Hare had run right over the top of the hill before Tortoise had even reached it.

After a while, Hare stopped to wait for Tortoise to come along. He began to feel sleepy. "Tortoise is so slow," he said to himself. "I'll just take a quick nap in this soft grass, and I'll finish the race later." He yawned and closed his eyes.

Meanwhile, Tortoise trudged on. He didn't need to stop for a rest. He eventually passed Hare, who was sound asleep in the grass. Tortoise smiled and walked quietly by.

After Hare had been asleep for quite a long time, he awoke with a start. Hare leaped to his feet and started running with all his strength toward the finish line. But it was too late! The race was over. Tortoise had won!

Hare felt very silly and was ashamed of himself. Imagine that, he thought, a hare being beaten by a tortoise!

Why did Tortoise beat Hare?

Practice the Skill

Predict Outcomes

1. How would Tortoise have described his day?

_____

_____

2. What might Tortoise say to Hare after winning the race?

_____

_____

Lesson of the Story

If Hare said, "I've learned an important lesson today," what would that lesson be?

_____

_____

_____

Vocabulary

What does "ran like the wind" mean?

_____

_____

_____

_____

The Ant and the Grasshopper

One summer day, a grasshopper was hopping around, chirping and singing to his heart's content. An ant passed by, carrying a long kernel of wheat to his nest.

How do you know the ant was preparing for winter?

"Why not come and play with me instead of working so hard?" asked the grasshopper.

"I'm collecting food now," said the ant. "I recommend that you do the same."

"Why bother?" asked the grasshopper. "We have plenty of food at the moment!"

"Suit yourself," replied the ant. The ant continued his work and the grasshopper leaped merrily away.

When winter came, the grasshopper had no food and was very hungry. I think I'll pay a visit to that little ant, he thought. He probably has plenty of food.

When the ant saw the starving grasshopper, he felt sorry for him. "I will help you this time," he said, "but next summer, you had better chirp, sing, and work!"

Practice the Skill

Conclude and Predict

Finish the sentences.

1. The ant is _____ but the grasshopper is

    _____ .

2. In winter, the ant _____

    _____ .

3. In winter, the grasshopper _____

    _____ .

4. Next summer, the grasshopper will probably _____

    _____ .

Lesson of the Story

If the grasshopper said, "I've learned an important lesson today," what would that lesson be?

_____

_____

Unit 5

Fact and Opinion   A fact is information that is true, and an opinion is what someone thinks or believes.

Sunny Waters

What do you think are the best things about living at Sunny Waters?

Are you tired of looking for your dream home? Are you starting to think it doesn't exist? Well, think again! Your dream home does exist, and it's waiting for you here at beautiful Sunny Waters.

Sunny Waters is only ninety-nine miles from the city! There's nothing here but houses and lots of lovely trees. You'll love the peace and quiet!

At Sunny Waters, you will step outside your front gate onto the shores of your sparkling neighborhood lake. At Sunny Waters, you can have boating and fishing and swimming right at your front door!

You'll never be alone at Sunny Waters. All your friends will want to visit when you live in this wonderful place! And it's easy for them to get here. Trains and buses travel to Sunny Waters every day.

8 AM	45	0
7 AM		0
6 AM		

VIA METROPOLITAN TRANSIT

Call now, and we'll send you our full-color brochure along with our price list. The minute you open the brochure, you'll love what you see.

Come to Sunny Waters today. Your dream home is waiting for you. Just look for the sign with the smiling swimmers!

Practice the Skill

Facts and Opinions

List three facts and three opinions about Sunny Waters.

Facts

- _____
- _____
- _____

Opinions

- _____
- _____
- _____

Compare and Contrast

1. Write two things that are the same about Sunny
   Waters and where you live. Then write two things
   that are different.

Same

- _____
- _____

Different

- _____
- _____

2. Now draw one of the similarities or differences listed on page 62.

Writing

How would you describe your dream home? Create your own brochure.

Glass: Let's Save It!

I collect glass jars and bottles. I keep marbles, polished stones, pencils, and pens in glass jars. I even have a plant that is growing in a glass bottle! I think everyone would enjoy collecting glass.

Why does the author believe it is wrong to throw glass away?

I think glass is the most beautiful material in the world. It does not wear out or rust. If you ask me, glass is much better than plastic. Many useful things are made from glass, like windows, light bulbs, and mirrors. Also, many of the things that are made from glass can be reused. For instance, empty jars and bottles can be filled and refilled. They can also be recycled.

I think glass is fantastic. But did you know that most families throw out five or six glass jars or bottles each week? I believe that these people are wasteful.

Glass that has been thrown away can be very dangerous. Broken glass sometimes ends up on beaches. People and animals can cut themselves on it. Broken glass that has been left lying in the sun causes the ground to heat up. This can make grass and leaves catch fire.

Please, next time you use glass, don't just throw it away. Collect it! Reuse it! Recycle it!

Recycle it! Collect it! Reuse it!

GLASS BOTTLES
GLASS BOTTLES

PAPER

PLASTIC BOTTLES
ALUMINUM CANS

Practice the Skill

Two Facts, Two Opinions

Write two of each from the text.

Facts

- _____
- _____

Opinions

- _____
- _____

Just Facts

List facts from the text.

Glass →

Useful things
made
from glass
_____
_____
_____

Dangers of
glass
_____
_____

Things you can
do with glass jars
and bottles
_____
_____

In My Opinion

1. In my opinion, bottles are best made of _____

   because _____

   _____ .

2. In my opinion, the most interesting facts about glass and

   plastic are _____

   _____ .

Main Idea

Check the main idea of the text.

☐ The author thinks glass is wonderful.

☐ Everyone would enjoy collecting glass.

Vocabulary

Recycle means "use again."
Can you find two other words where *re-* means "again"?
Write the words and their meanings.

_____

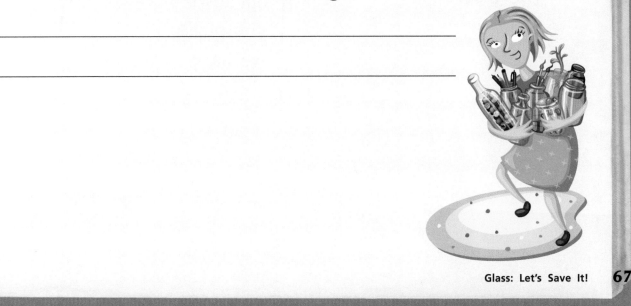

_____

The Daily Spin

What opinions does Mr. Sullivan use to support his plan?

Yesterday afternoon, Mr. Harry Sullivan went to South Elementary School to have a discussion with the students. Mr. Sullivan plans to dig up Oak Tree Park and build a mall on the site. Our reporter recorded the discussion.

Anne: Why can't you find somewhere else to build your mall, Mr. Sullivan?

Mr. Sullivan: Now, you shouldn't question decisions that are made by adults. Every town needs stores. I think Oak Tree Park is a huge waste of space. It is the perfect place for a mall.

Anne: We think there are enough places to shop in our town already. Will you please listen to what we have to say?

Mr. Sullivan: Of course. Everybody knows I always listen to what other people say! But I'm sure you'll soon realize I'm right.

Tyler: All of us think the oak trees in our park are beautiful. Oak trees take a long, long time to grow. They start out as tiny acorns. When they grow older, they give us a lot of shade. Please don't chop them down!

Mr. Sullivan: You won't need shade when you're in the mall. It will have a big roof. If you ask me, old oak trees are ugly and messy. Trees just get in the way of important things like malls.

Lynette: We all need trees, Mr. Sullivan. Trees keep the air clean and the planet healthy.

Mr. Sullivan: Yes, yes, I know we need some trees. But I think your park is getting in the way of progress. You won't miss it once it's gone.

Miles: We believe the park is for everyone. Kids need exercise. Dogs need exercise. Even our moms and dads need exercise. Exercise keeps us all healthy and happy. Please leave our beautiful park alone.

The discussion ended here. The children returned to class. Mr. Sullivan was exhausted, so he went to the park and sat on a bench to rest.

The Daily Spin would like you to tell us what you think. Why are parks and trees important? We'd love to hear from you.

Practice the Skill

Fact or Opinion?

Write "F" for fact or "O" for opinion in each box.

The park is a waste of space. ☐
Old oak trees are ugly. ☐
The mall will be under one big roof. ☐
Oak trees give shade. ☐
The park is the perfect place for the mall. ☐
Dogs need exercise. ☐

Two Facts, Two Opinions

Think about a park or playground you have visited recently. Write two facts and two opinions about it.

Facts

• _____

• _____

Opinions

• _____

• _____

Writing

Write a letter to *The Daily Spin* about why parks and trees are important.

That's Rubbish!

What facts does Woody B. Kleen use to support his opinion?

Piney Acres Campground
Anywhere, U.S.A.

To Whom It May Concern:

I have just returned from a camping vacation at Piney Acres. I will never go back there again! People were throwing their litter onto the ground. I was shocked that the campground was so dirty. I think your campers must be the most careless people in the world!

I believe people who drop litter onto the ground and into lakes and rivers don't care about nature. Litter can harm fish, birds, and small animals. Broken glass that is left on the ground can even cause forest fires!

I think people who litter should be banned from Piney Acres and all other campgrounds. You must tell your campers to think about litter. It is pollution, and pollution is bad for our planet! It is one of the biggest problems in the world today. What are you going to do about it?

Thank you for your time.

Woody B. Kleen

Practice the Skill

Piney Acres Facts and Opinions

List three facts and three opinions from the letter.

Facts	Opinions
1. _____	1. _____
_____	_____
_____	_____
2. _____	2. _____
_____	_____
_____	_____
3. _____	3. _____
_____	_____
_____	_____

Check Comprehension

1. What were people doing with their litter?

_____

_____

2. Why is broken glass dangerous?

_____

_____

Unit 6

Cause and Effect A cause is why something happens, and an effect is the result.

How to Celebrate

Why would a street party be a good way to celebrate Independence Day?

June 1, 2006

On July 4, 1776, the United States won its independence and became a free nation. Every year on July 4, Americans celebrate Independence Day. A neighborhood party is a great way to celebrate the occasion. With organization and hard work, you can have the best party in town!

First, get permission from the local police department to close off some of the streets in your neighborhood. That way, passing cars won't interrupt your activities, and everyone will be safe.

Advertise your party. Post signs on bulletin boards and in shop windows. Make invitations and deliver them to every house in the neighborhood. That way, everyone will know about the party!

the Fourth of July

Provide entertainment! Everyone can help organize games and music. If there are fun things to do, people will stay at the party longer and enjoy themselves more.

Every party needs food. If you have a potluck, people can bring their favorite dishes to share. That way, there will be a variety of yummy things to eat.

Enjoy the games, music, and food as you wait for the sun to go down. Then gather with your friends and neighbors to watch beautiful fireworks fill up the sky! Your party will be the best in town!

Practice the Skill

Cause and Effect

Fill in the missing effects.

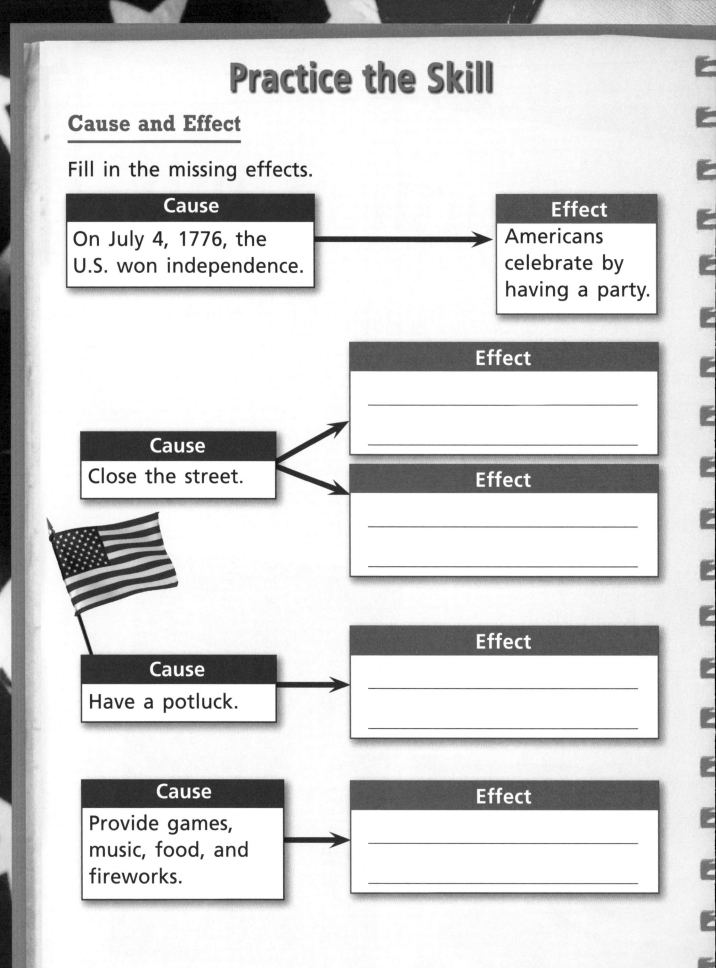

Cause

On July 4, 1776, the U.S. won independence.

Effect

Americans celebrate by having a party.

Effect

_____

_____

Cause

Close the street.

Effect

_____

_____

Cause

Have a potluck.

Effect

_____

_____

Cause

Provide games, music, food, and fireworks.

Effect

_____

_____

Have a Party!

To organize a neighborhood party, people need to do many things. Read what needs to be done and write the reason.

Get permission to close off street.

Reason: _____

_____

Make signs and invitations.

Reason: _____

_____

Provide entertainment.

Reason: _____

_____

Vocabulary

In the first paragraph, find

- a word with two syllables _____

- a word with three syllables _____

- a word with four syllables _____

- a word with five syllables _____

A Terrible Mess

What problems did the messy bedroom cause?

"Clean up your bedroom," my mom said to me,
So I tried to open the door.
I pushed and I pushed, but I couldn't get in,
There was no room to move on the floor!

"I cannot open the door," I exclaimed,
"My clothing is blocking the way.
And a bad smell is coming from inside my drawer.
It's a cheese slice, all moldy and gray!"

I thought I heard scrambling, rustles, and squeaks—
It made my hair stand up on end.
Did a mouse like the smell of that stinky old cheese?
Had he come for a feast with a friend?

"Never leave a big mess," my mother had warned,
"Or your bedroom will fill up with mice."
I didn't believe her. I hadn't cleaned up,
And now I am paying the price!

I came back with a box of gigantic trash bags,
And I started to tackle the task.
By the time I had picked up my smelly old socks,
I wanted to put on a mask.

I tidied my books and my sneakers and clothes,
And I cleaned up my closet and shelf.
Now I can cartwheel all over the floor,
And I'm ever so pleased with myself!

Practice the Skill

Cause and Effect

Fill in the missing causes and effects.

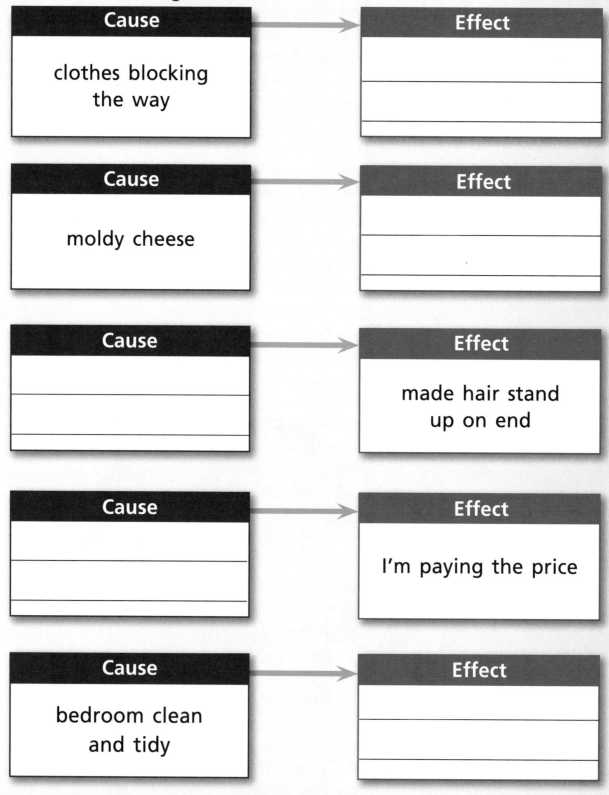

Cause	Effect
clothes blocking the way	

Cause	Effect
moldy cheese	

Cause	Effect
	made hair stand up on end

Cause	Effect
	I'm paying the price

Cause	Effect
bedroom clean and tidy	

Drawing Conclusions about Mom

Do you think this is the first time the child's mom has said,

"Clean up your bedroom"? _____ Why do you think so?

_____

_____

Messy or Not?

Draw a picture of what you think the bedroom will look like
in two weeks.

Why do you think the room will look like this?

_____

_____

Forgetful Sam

Do you ever forget things? My brother Sam forgets things all the time. Once when we went fishing, Sam forgot his fishing rod. He tied some fishing line to a long stick and said he'd use that. But he forgot to tie a hook on the end so it didn't work!

I caught five fish that day, but Sam didn't catch anything. He forgot to watch his stick! He put it down on a rock and then ran off to chase a dragonfly. The stick slid off the rock, fell into the water, and floated away.

What happened after Sam forgot to close the door to Izzy's hutch?

Mom and Dad gave Sam a rabbit for his birthday. "You'll have to take good care of her," said Mom. "You'll have to feed her and give her water every day," said Dad.

"Don't worry," said Sam. "I promise I'll never forget."

Sam named his rabbit Izzy. Every morning, he fed Izzy and gave her plenty of water. Every afternoon, he took her out to play. Sam took great care of his new pet.

One day, Sam was grooming Izzy's soft brown coat. She hated it! She twitched the whole time. When Sam put her back in her hutch, Izzy scratched him.

Sam ran off to clean up his scratch. He forgot to close the door to Izzy's hutch. When Sam went back, Izzy was gone.

"Izzy!" he shouted. "Where are you?"

I came out to help Sam search. We looked in the garden. No Izzy! We looked under the house. No Izzy! Sam was worried sick. "Poor Izzy," he said. "She'll be so scared!"

Then we heard a crunching sound. "Look!" said Sam. Izzy was sitting on the porch, happily eating a carrot.

"Dad must have dropped a carrot when he brought in the groceries!" said Sam.

"That was lucky," I said. "If it wasn't for that carrot, Izzy might have run away!"

Sam picked up Izzy and gave her a big hug. "I can't believe I left your door open. I'll never, ever let it happen again!" he said. Izzy just kept on munching.

That afternoon, Sam tied a bright red string to the door of Izzy's hutch. He said the string would always remind him to check that the door was shut. It worked—Izzy hasn't escaped since! Sam is still forgetful about some things, but when it comes to Izzy, his memory is just fine!

Practice the Skill

Chain Reactions

Here is an example of an effect becoming a cause:

Cause	Effect
Sam forgets things all the time.	He forgot his fishing rod.

Cause → **Effect**
He made his own fishing rod.

Fill in the missing causes and effects.

Cause	Effect
Sam went to clean his scratch.	_____ _____ _____ .

Cause → **Effect**
_____ _____ _____ .

Cause	Effect
Dad dropped a carrot.	Izzy stopped to eat it.

Cause → **Effect**
_____ _____ .

Cause → **Effect**
_____ _____ _____ .

Splat!

What caused Liz to need help?

This morning, I made breakfast for my big sister, Liz. A smoothie seemed like a good idea. First, I put fresh strawberries in the blender and turned it on. Whoosh! Strawberry mush went everywhere!

"You forgot the lid!" exclaimed Liz. "I think I should help."

"No, thanks," I said.

Next, I mixed the pancake batter. I put two eggs on the counter. "Watch out!" yelled Liz. It was too late. The eggs rolled onto the floor. Plop! Plop! The eggs smashed.

"I think I should help," said Liz.

"No, thanks," I said.

Finally, I was ready to cook the pancakes. I poured the batter into a pan. When the first side was done, I flipped the pancake high into the air. It landed neatly back in the pan.

"Wow!" said Liz. "Can I try?"

I stood back. My sister hurled the pancake into the air. It didn't flip. It just kept on going up. Splat! It hit the ceiling and stuck fast.

"I think I should help," I said.

"Yes, please!" said Liz.

Practice the Skill

Missing Causes and Effects

Fill in the boxes.

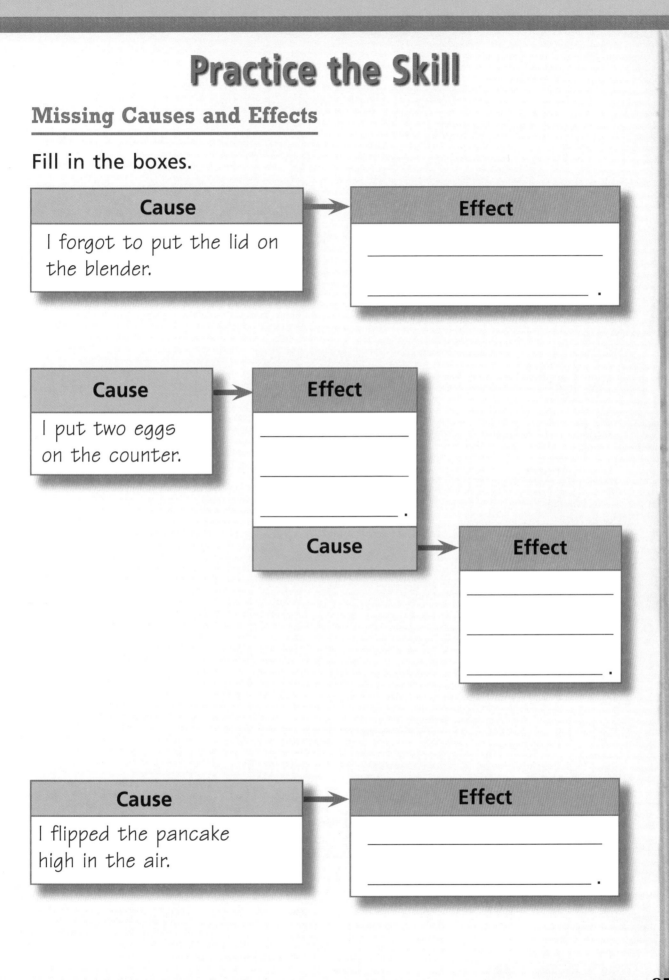

Cause
I forgot to put the lid on the blender.

Effect
_____
_____.

Cause
I put two eggs on the counter.

Effect
_____
_____
_____.

Cause

Effect
_____
_____
_____.

Cause
I flipped the pancake high in the air.

Effect
_____
_____.

Acknowledgments

Illustrations
Rae Dale, pp. 18, 19, 20; Janine Dawson, pp. 34, 36–39, 86; Andrea Jaretzki, pp. 60, 83 (background); Julie Knoblock, pp. 64, 67, 82, 83, 84; Celina Korcak, pp. 12, 14, 15, 78, 79; Vasya Korman, pp. 46, 47, 49, 50, 51, 52, 54, 55, 56, 57, 58, 59.

Photographs
Australian Picture Library, cover, pp. 5, 7, 16, 19, 23, 27, 30, 40 (bottom), 61 (top left); Coo-ee Pictures, pp. 4, 22, 25, 40 (background), 41, 42, (background), 43, 61 (right), 69, 71, 72; Gary Crabbe, pp. 16 (bottom left), 17; John and Claude Elks, pp. 8–9; Getty Images, pp. 26, 28, 29; Gibson Stock, p. 65; Great Southern Stock/Philip Game, p. 42; photolibrary.com, p. 44 (top); *San Francisco Chronicle*, pp. 13, 30 (background); Sporting Images, p. 44 (bottom); The Bancroft Library, pp. 8, 10.